W9-CHR-498

GREAT BASKETBALL

BY ANDRES YBARRA

DEBATES

GREAT
SPORTS
DEBATES

SportsZone

An Imprint of Abdo Publishing | abdopublishing.com

ABDOPUBLISHING.COM

Published by Abdo Publishing, a division of ABDO, PO Box 398166, Minneapolis, Minnesota 55439.
Copyright © 2019 by Abdo Consulting Group, Inc. International copyrights reserved in all countries.
No part of this book may be reproduced in any form without written permission from the publisher.
SportsZone™ is a trademark and logo of Abdo Publishing.

Printed in the United States of America, North Mankato, Minnesota
052018
092018

Cover Photo: Doug Pizac/AP Images, right; Lennox Mclendon/AP Images, left
Interior Photos: Matt York/AP Images, 4–5; Susan Ragan/AP Images, 6, 34–35; John Gaps III/AP Images,
9; Eric Gay/AP Images, 10–11; Rick Bowmer/AP Images, 12–13; Frank Franklin II/AP Images, 14, 23; Fred
Jewell/AP Images, 17; James Crisp/AP Images, 18; Kevin Reece/AP Images, 20–21; George Tiedemann/
Sports Illustrated/Getty Images, 25; Beth A. Keiser/AP Images, 26–27; Charles Bennett/AP Images, 28; Ron
Schwane/AP Images, 29; Lenny Ignelzi/AP Images, 30; Gene Herrick/AP Images, 33; William Straeter/AP
Images, 36; Bryant/AP Images, 37; Jessica Hill/AP Images, 38–39; Jordan Murph/Sports Illustrated/Getty
Images, 42; John Peterson/AP Images, 44; Arena Creative/Shutterstock Images, 45

Editor: Julie Dick
Series Designer: Laura Polzin

Library of Congress Control Number: 2017961930

Publisher's Cataloging-in-Publication Data

Names: Ybarra, Andres, author.
Title: Great basketball debates / by Andres Ybarra.
Description: Minneapolis, Minnesota : Abdo Publishing, 2019. | Series: Great sports debates | Includes
online resources and index.
Identifiers: ISBN 9781532114427 (lib.bdg.) | ISBN 9781532154256 (ebook)
Subjects: LCSH: Basketball players--Juvenile literature. | Basketball--Records--United States--Juvenile
literature. | Sports--History--Juvenile literature. | Debates and debating--Juvenile literature.
Classification: DDC 796.323--dc23

TABLE OF CONTENTS

Carmelo Anthony throws down a dunk
for Team USA at the 2016 Olympics.

CHAPTER ONE

TEAM USA: PRO OR COLLEGE PLAYERS?

It's hard today to imagine Olympic basketball without players from the National Basketball Association (NBA) and Women's National Basketball Association (WNBA). But the best players in the world weren't always allowed to participate in the Olympics. Until 1989 USA Basketball—the governing body for all teams that represent the country in international play—did not allow professionals to compete. Instead college players filled the rosters of all US basketball teams. Given that the United States

The 1988 US men's Olympic team was the last to be made up of college players.

was the lone world power in the sport, they usually had plenty of success in international competition.

At the 1988 Summer Olympics, the eligibility restrictions were loosened and countries were allowed to have professionals play on their teams. The United States still fielded a team of college players. The US team finished a disappointing third in the men's tournament. After that humiliating bronze medal, USA Basketball decided to start sending NBA players to international tournaments. The change began with the "Dream Team" at the 1992 Barcelona Games. A US team that included many future Hall of Famers, including Michael Jordan, Magic Johnson, and Larry Bird, dominated the competition. The Dream Team was the biggest story of the Olympics that year.

But should professionals be allowed to play in international competition? Was the change good for the sport? Or should

YOUNG STARS

In 1980 USA Basketball assembled its youngest men's national team ever, but it didn't take part in the Summer Olympics. The United States boycotted those games because the Soviet Union, which was hosting the Games, had recently invaded Afghanistan. Instead, the team played exhibition games against five NBA all-star teams. The national team only

USA Basketball go back to allowing only amateur athletes to compete?

When the modern Olympics were founded in 1896, they were meant to be an amateur competition. Over the years, some athletes were even stripped of their medals when it was discovered that they had competed professionally. Officials eventually changed the rules, swayed by the marketing potential of famous professional athletes. But the change doesn't apply equally to all sports. Athletes in sports such as gymnastics and swimming aren't paid to compete in leagues the way professional basketball players are. Some Olympic purists believe that's what makes the Games special. They don't think wealthy professional athletes represent the Olympic ideal.

Others also argue that allowing pros to play makes the American team too dominant. Even before the Dream Team era, the US men's team won nine gold medals, one silver, and one bronze in the 11 Olympic tournaments in which it participated. Since 1992, both men's and women's teams have won gold in six of seven Games. And not only do US Olympic teams win, they win big. In 2012 the US men outscored opponents by a combined 191 points in five games in the opening rounds.

John Stockton, Chris Mullin, and Charles Barkley were members of the 1992 Dream Team.

The domination extends to the women's team as well.
In the 2016 Games, the US women rolled to the gold medal
by winning all eight of their games. And their average
margin of victory was 37.2 points. But the Olympics are also

The US women's team won gold at the 2016 Rio Olympics.

an opportunity to highlight the world's best athletes. The international competition is meant to feature the best of the best. Some supporters argue that it's wrong to exclude elite athletes in a certain sport just because they are professionals.

Others think it's good to allow NBA players to compete internationally because it raises interest in the league. In 2016, a record 46 NBA players participated in the Rio Olympics, representing 10 different countries.

Kevin Garnett (21) was the first player in 20 years to enter the NBA straight out of high school.

CHAPTER TWO

SHOULD HIGH SCHOOL PLAYERS BE ABLE TO TURN PRO?

As of 2017, NBA teams could only draft players who were at least 19 years old or whose high school class had been graduated for a year. The minimum age for draft eligibility was brought up again between the National Basketball Players Association (NBPA) and team owners. This reignited a debate on whether high schoolers are too young for the NBA.

Gerald Green (5) joined the Boston Celtics straight out of high school in 2005.

Beginning in 1971, a player as young as 17 could enter the NBA Draft if he demonstrated a financial hardship—in other words, if his family needed his salary to survive. Even with this exception, only two players were drafted straight out of high school in the next 25 years. NBA teams were reluctant to draft players without high-level experience.

Everything changed in 1995. That's when high school star Kevin Garnett announced he would enter the draft only a few weeks after graduating. The Minnesota Timberwolves selected him with the fifth pick of the NBA Draft, and Garnett went on to become a 15-time All-Star. Other future NBA All-Stars, such as Kobe Bryant, Tracy McGrady, and LeBron James, followed the same path. But in 2006, the league changed the rule and mandated that players be at least 19 years old or out of high school for one year before entering the draft.

Those who agree with the rule say most high school students aren't ready to play against bigger, stronger, and more experienced players. Many people think young players should take advantage of the opportunity to gain experience while also attending college, rather than sit on an NBA bench.

Cincinnati's Kenyon Martin was the No. 1 pick in the 2000 NBA Draft. He was the last No. 1 pick to play four years of college basketball. Martin played for five teams over 15 NBA seasons, averaging 12.3 points and 6.8 rebounds per game.

Even stars such as McGrady and Tyson Chandler needed a few years before they succeeded. Gerald Green, drafted by the Boston Celtics in 2005, was one of the last high school players to go straight into the NBA. However, he supports an age restriction so that players can develop at the college level.

Not every high school player drafted became a star. Garnett, James, and Bryant made big impacts right away. But others like Kwame Brown, Sebastian Telfair, and Ndudi Ebi became known for their disastrous attempts to play in the NBA straight out of high school. They made their money in the short term, but many people believe that skipping college stunted their development and shortened their careers.

Supporters of the age limit argue that more players who aren't ready for the league will be drafted if the limit is removed.

Kenyon Martin (4) was drafted by the New Jersey Nets after playing for four years at the University of Cincinnati.

The Minnesota Timberwolves drafted Karl-Anthony Towns out of the University of Kentucky with the first pick in 2015.

After all, players are drafted based on their potential, and it's a much bigger risk to properly evaluate the potential of a 17-year-old playing against high schoolers versus a 21-year-old playing against college players. Former NBA commissioner

David Stern has repeatedly said he wants to protect teams from making those mistakes.

But opponents of the age limit argue that it's not fair to say that no high school players are ready for the NBA. For instance, 39 players were drafted straight out of high school between 1995 and 2005. Of those players, 10 became NBA All-Stars. This is why opponents of the limit argue players should be allowed to enter the NBA if teams believe them to be ready.

Support for the age restriction also comes from those who think that drafting high school players is bad for college basketball. But some believe the new rule actually harms college basketball more than it helps. The rule accidentally created a "one-and-done" system. Some players join college teams for one season before leaving for the NBA. This makes it hard for college coaches to build solid teams that have experience playing together. That's just one of many factors the NBA must consider when trying to decide the best way to handle this issue.

CHAPTER
THREE

SHOULD THE DRAFT LOTTERY BE ELIMINATED?

Professional football and baseball have a simple process for drafting new players. In those leagues, each round begins with the team that had the worst record the year before. The team with the second-worst record gets the next pick, and so on. This system gives less successful teams a better chance to improve.

UNLIKELY ODDS

The Chicago Bulls had one of the most unlikely draft lottery wins ever when they came away with the No. 1 pick in 2008. That year the Bulls had only a 1.7 percent chance to secure the top pick. They used the pick on guard Derrick Rose, who won the Most Valuable Player award and became a three-time All-Star in seven seasons in Chicago.

But the NBA does it differently. Every year 16 teams make the playoffs. The rest of the teams enter a lottery system that assigns a number of ping-pong balls to each of them. Then the balls are randomly drawn to determine the draft order. The team with the worst record has more balls than others. That means it has a better chance to receive the No. 1 pick. But it doesn't always work out that way.

Many basketball fans think the lottery is exciting. They watch live coverage to see who ends up in which position. Critics believe the lottery can hurt the quality of play. It sometimes appears that nonplayoff teams intentionally lose games at the end of the season to get more ping-pong balls in the lottery. This is called "tanking." This gives teams a better chance to win

NBA deputy commissioner Mark Tatum informs Boston Celtics co-owner Wyc Grousbeck that the Celtics had won the 2017 draft lottery.

the top pick. Teams may sometimes do this by losing games while resting their best players, even when they're healthy.

A recent rule change was made to discourage tanking. Previously, the team with the league's worst record had a 25 percent chance to win the No. 1 pick. But in 2017, the NBA announced changes. The new system gives the team that finishes with the worst record only a 14 percent chance at winning the top pick. The teams with the second- and third-worst records would also have a 14 percent chance to win.

On the other hand, some people think that all nonplayoff teams should have equal odds to win the top pick. That was the case in 1985 when the NBA held its first draft lottery. That year, the New York Knicks won the lottery, even though they had the third-worst record in the league. They went on to select star center Patrick Ewing. Some critics of the lottery system believe the NBA wanted Ewing to go to New York because it would help draw more attention to the league.

At that time, the NBA used envelopes instead of ping-pong balls. A rumor started that the Knicks' envelope was placed in a freezer so that NBA commissioner David Stern could feel which envelope to choose. Other conspiracy theories exist, but there's no evidence any of them are true. Still some people refer to these rumors to question whether the draft lottery system should be eliminated.

NBA commissioner David Stern draws an envelope at the first NBA draft lottery in 1985.

Phil Jackson celebrates with Michael Jordan after the Chicago Bulls won the 1996 NBA championship.

CHAPTER
FOUR

MJ & PHIL: ARE THEY REALLY THE GREATEST?

Many people believe Michael Jordan is the greatest basketball player ever. His longtime Chicago Bulls coach, Phil Jackson, is often called the greatest coach.

Jordan was a six-time NBA champion who never lost in an NBA Finals series. He was a five-time NBA MVP, a six-time NBA Finals MVP, a 10-time league scoring

27

champion, and a 14-time NBA All-Star. He helped make the NBA one of the world's most popular sports leagues.

Jackson was courtside for all six of Jordan's titles in Chicago. Then Jackson moved on to Los Angeles, where he won five more championships coaching the Lakers. No NBA coach has won more titles.

Still, many other players and coaches can challenge Jordan and Jackson to their "best-ever" titles. LeBron James

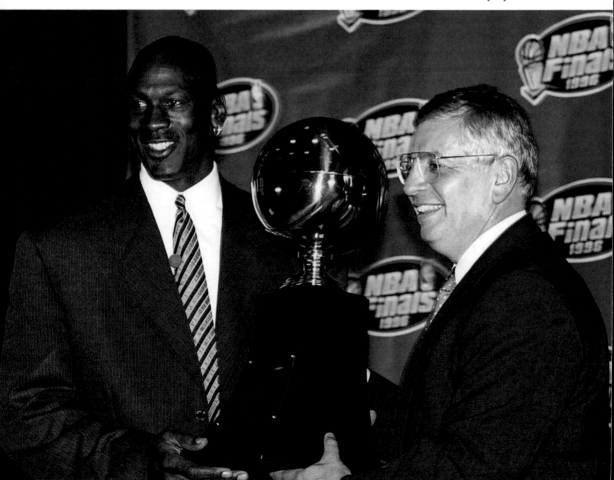

Michael Jordan shows off his 1996 NBA MVP trophy.

LeBron James became a fixture in the NBA Finals.

frequently draws comparisons to Jordan. He led his team to

the NBA Finals eight times through 2017, but he only won three

championships. Still James reached the finals seven years in a

row, something Jordan never did. Jordan averaged nearly three

points a game more than James. But James is the better 3-point

shooter, rebounder, and passer. People say James is a better all-around player because he involves his teammates, whereas Jordan was more of a do-it-yourself type of player.

Another challenger to Jordan's throne is Kareem Abdul-Jabbar, who played for 20 NBA seasons. He scored more career points than any other player. He was named to the Hall of Fame in 1995. Both men won six titles and made the All-NBA First Team 10 times. Abdul-Jabbar has one more regular-season MVP award than Jordan. Some Abdul-Jabbar fans argue he was a greater player because he turned bad teams into champions earlier in his career. Jordan didn't win a title until he teamed with another star player, Scottie Pippen.

And if titles measure greatness, perhaps Bill Russell should be considered the best player of all time. After all, he won 11 of them in his 13-year career, compared to Jordan's six.

In 2009 the Los Angeles Lakers defeated the Orlando Magic in the NBA Finals. That victory moved Jackson past Boston's Red Auerbach for the most NBA titles of any coach. Jackson won one more championships before retiring. Many people think those two extra titles give Jackson a leg up in the

Kareem Abdul-Jabbar shows off his deadly skyhook.

A COACH'S OPINION

In his prime, Kobe Bryant often drew comparisons to Michael Jordan. Who better to settle the debate between Jordan vs. Bryant than Phil Jackson, the man who coached them both? In a 2013 interview with *Sports Illustrated*, Jackson said that Jordan was the better leader, shooter, and defender.

"greatest coach" conversation, while others think Auerbach's accomplishments are more impressive.

One area in which Auerbach beats Jackson is consecutive titles. Jackson had three separate streaks of three consecutive titles. Jackson's longest streak was six titles in a row. Auerbach won eight straight with the Celtics. In fact, Auerbach is the only coach in NBA history with eight or more titles in less than 15 years. Jackson's critics also point out that he took 20 years to win nine titles. Auerbach did it in 14.

The most common argument against Jackson's greatness is that he only won because he leaned on superstars like Jordan, Pippen, Kobe Bryant, and Shaquille O'Neal. Auerbach also coached all-time greats such as Russell, Bob Cousy, and John Havlicek. But only Russell is commonly mentioned as one of the greatest ever. Auerbach was also more involved with assembling his team's roster as a Celtics executive.

The Boston Celtics carry coach Red Auerbach off the court after sweeping the NBA Finals in 1959.

But is it fair to criticize Jackson for having great players on his team? His supporters point out that it wasn't easy to successfully manage the big egos of his superstars. Not just any coach could have done that.

THE BEST OF COLLEGE AND PRO

D uke is widely considered one of the greatest college
basketball programs of all time. Through 2018 the
Blue Devils had won five NCAA championships since 1991. But
Duke lost the 1989–90 national title by 30 points. The team
that beat them? The University of Nevada–Las Vegas (UNLV)
Runnin' Rebels. Those Rebels seemed unstoppable a year later.
They won 34 straight games, but they couldn't finish the season
unbeaten. They lost to Duke by two in the Final Four.

They were two great teams, to be sure. But neither is generally considered to be the greatest ever. Instead, many fans point to the run put together by the University of California, Los Angeles (UCLA). From 1966 to 1968 center Lew Alcindor (later to be known as Kareem Abdul-Jabbar) and the Bruins went 59–1 and won two national titles. Four years later, they went undefeated and won another title.

Bill Russell (6) led the University of San Francisco to an undefeated championship season in 1955–56.

Louisiana Tech was a power in the early days of women's basketball.

But even the mighty Bruins weren't the first team to win an undefeated championship. That distinction belongs to the University of San Francisco in 1955–56. Led by player Bill Russell, the Dons went 29–0 for the first-ever perfect season.

The University of Connecticut Huskies went undefeated in back-to-back seasons, 2008–09 and 2009–10.

Debating the greatest women's college team is even tougher. That's because several teams over the years have seemed invincible.

Louisiana Tech won the first women's National Collegiate Athletic Association (NCAA) title in 1982. The Lady Techsters

were ranked No. 1 every single week that season. They won 54
straight games between that season and the next. In fact, the
program was 320–29 in the 1980s.

But could they have beaten the 1986 Texas Longhorns?
That team went 34–0 as the first women's team to complete

SUPERTEAMS

When LeBron James left his hometown Cleveland Cavaliers in 2010 to join fellow superstars Dwyane Wade and Chris Bosh in Miami, the era of the "superteam" was born. Definitions of a super team vary. Generally speaking, a superteam has three or more big-name players. And some of those players had success elsewhere before joining their new team.

a perfect season. Although Texas is one of the country's most successful programs, the 1986 team remains the only one in Longhorn history to win an NCAA title.

As great as Louisiana Tech and Texas were in the 1980s, fans argue that two other programs are strong candidates for the greatest of all time. The Tennessee Volunteers of the 1990s make a strong case. Coached by the legendary Pat Summitt, Tennessee won three straight titles from 1996 to 1998, capping the run with a 39–0 season.

However, Tennessee wasn't the last team to achieve a perfect season. The University of Connecticut (UConn) Huskies did it in 2002. And then UConn had two more perfect seasons on their way to a record 111–game win streak.

On the professional side, perhaps the greatest NBA fantasy series of all time would be between the 1995–96 Chicago Bulls and the 2015–16 Golden State Warriors. Led by Michael Jordan, Scottie Pippen, and Dennis Rodman, the Bulls set an NBA record by finishing the regular season with 72 wins and only 10 losses. Chicago won its first 37 home games. They also won a record 33 road games.

For 20 years, many people thought the Bulls' record could never be matched. But on April 10, 2016, Golden State won its 72nd game by beating San Antonio. Three days later, the Warriors broke the Bulls' record by defeating Memphis to finish the regular season 73–9. The Warriors were also the first team in NBA history to avoid losing back-to-back games the entire regular season.

But there's one reason some still think the Bulls were a better team: they won the NBA title the year they set the record. The Warriors? They lost to LeBron James and the Cleveland Cavaliers in a tense seven-game NBA Finals.

Of all the great basketball teams over the ages, one team stands out as seemingly impossible to beat. The 1992 US Olympic men's team started a new era of international

basketball with the inclusion of NBA stars. No one stood a chance against them.

The team was loaded with some of the greatest players in NBA history. Aside from Jordan, Magic Johnson, and Larry Bird, the team also included Pippen, Charles Barkley, David Robinson, Clyde Drexler, Karl Malone, and John Stockton. In eight Olympic games, the US team won every game by at least 32 points. Croatia came the closest, losing 117–85 in the gold medal game in Barcelona, Spain.

While future US men's teams were called "Dream Team 2," "Dream Team 3," and so on, most people like to say there was only one true Dream Team. Could any other team have ever beaten them?

The Golden State Warriors set a new record for victories in a season in 2015–16, breaking the Chicago Bulls' record set in 1995–96.

TOPICS FOR FURTHER
DISCUSSION

- Is March Madness too demanding for players?

- Which is more exciting to watch: college basketball, the NBA, or the WNBA?

- Should high school games feature a shot clock?

- How much should the WNBA pay players?

- Should players be allowed to dunk the ball?

- Who was the best NBA player to never win a championship?

- Do three-point shots unbalance the game?

• **Should the baskets be raised to make the game more challenging?**

GLOSSARY

AMATEUR
Someone who is not paid to perform an activity.

BOYCOTT
Refusing to take part in an event as a form of protest.

COMMISSIONER
The chief executive of a sports league.

CONSECUTIVE
Following each other without interruption.

CONSPIRACY
A secret plan to break the rules.

DRAFT
A system that allows teams to acquire new players coming into a league.

ELIMINATE
To completely remove something.

ERA
A period of time in history.

INTERNATIONAL
Involving athletes from several different countries.

LEAGUE
A group of teams that participate together in a sport.

PROFESSIONAL
A person who gets paid to perform.

ONLINE RESOURCES

Booklinks
NONFICTION NETWORK
FREE! ONLINE NONFICTION RESOURCES

To learn more about great basketball debates, visit **abdobooklinks.com**. These links are routinely monitored and updated to provide the most current information available.

MORE INFORMATION

BOOKS

Ervin, Phil. *Total Basketball*. Minneapolis, MN: Abdo Publishing, 2017.

Graves, Will. *The Best NBA Teams of All Time*. Minneapolis, MN: Abdo Publishing, 2015.

Williams, Doug. *Great Moments in Olympic Basketball*. Minneapolis, MN: Abdo Publishing, 2015.

INDEX

ABOUT THE AUTHOR

Andres "Andy" Ybarra is a public relations executive and freelance sports writer based in Minnesota. He has covered the Vikings, Twins, Timberwolves, and Wild, as well as University of Minnesota athletics. He lives in the Twin Cities with his wife and three children.